Are We Safer Now?

Are We Safer Now?

◆

Airline Security in a Post-9/11 Society

Byron L. Cherry, Sr., PhD

iUniverse, Inc.
New York Lincoln Shanghai

Are We Safer Now?
Airline Security in a Post-9/11 Society

Copyright © 2006 by Byron L. Cherry

iUniverse books may be ordered through booksellers or by contacting:

iUniverse
2021 Pine Lake Road, Suite 100
Lincoln, NE 68512
www.iuniverse.com
1-800-Authors (1-800-288-4677)

ISBN-13: 978-0-595-36398-8 (pbk)
ISBN-13: 978-0-595-80833-5 (ebk)
ISBN-10: 0-595-36398-9 (pbk)
ISBN-10: 0-595-80833-6 (ebk)

Printed in the United States of America

To my lovely wife—the mother of our three beautiful children—Josephine Benson Cherry. Her love, understanding, and patience allowed me to continue in this field of study. I am truly blessed to have her as a wife and partner for life. To our children—Byron II, Bryan, and Ashley—I say: keep making me smile as you do every day, and keep bringing the joy into my life. I also dedicate this book to my parents, Jean O. Cherry and the late Willie R. Cherry, Sr., for their belief in me as a child with a very vivid and wild imagination. They allowed me to pursue my dreams and goals as I grew up in Norfolk, Virginia. I want to pay special tribute to my parents-in-law, Josephine W. Benson and the late Ernest L. Benson, Sr., for allowing me to marry their daughter. God bless them all.

Contents

List of Tables

Acknowledgments

I would like to acknowledge first and foremost my Lord and Savior Jesus Christ. Philippians 4:13 states that "I can do all things through Christ who strengthens me" (New King James Version). It was with his strength and love that I was able to complete this book. I want to acknowledge the assistance and guidance of the members of my dissertation committee—Dr. Paul Carr, Dr. Gail Derrick, and Dr. Robert Dyer—for their support and humor throughout the writing process. My dissertation chair, Dr. Paul Carr (also known as "Alpha Dog"), was especially patient and understanding during this time. To my family and friends: thanks for your understanding during those moments when I was not the easiest person to get along with.

I would also like to acknowledge the superb support from my cohort group. We were always there for one another, and I could not have completed this book without their support and love.

In Matthew Henry's (2004) commentary on Ecclesiastes 12:12, he states that in this day men will write many books. They will write and publish until they are completely exhausted, but their instruction cannot replace what we get from the word of God.

1

Introduction

Overview

As the first flights began again on September 15, some crews refused to fly, not confident of airport security. Those who steeled themselves to work entered a strange new workplace. With no guidance from the airlines or the Federal Aviation Administration (FAA) on how to handle potential future hijackings, flight attendants inventoried galleys for objects they could use as defensive weapons. Shell-shocked passengers sometimes hugged flight attendants as they boarded. Many crewmembers barely contained tears, often hiding in galleys to avoid alarming passengers.

—Rodney Ward, May 2002
Association of Flight Attendants

As the growth in air traffic picks up again, people are demanding more safety and security. As we look back to the events of September 11, 2001, we realize that this is a day that most Americans will never forget. Some of those who witnessed and watched airplanes plunge into both World Trade Center buildings in New York and the Pentagon will have to live with those unforgettable memories for the rest of their lives. Many private citizens and commercial industries are still feeling the impact and aftermath of that dreadful day both emotionally and economically.

Airline safety and security are two of the most important issues facing this nation and the world today. *Airline safety* refers to the construction and maintenance taken to ensure airplanes are free from factors that may lead to the injury of passengers or crewmembers. *Airline security* is aimed at the prevention of illegal acts, including terrorism. Airline security efforts include intelligence gathering, pre-boarding procedures, and the watchful eyes of airport security personnel.

In a 2003 study while attending the National Defense University, Col. John Wassink and I, both students at the time showed that major increases in airline safety and security efforts are consistently implemented in response to successful terror attacks (see Table 1). Government direction and funding, which are generally required to enforce safety and security improvements, are more readily available after a successful terrorist attack. Further, while memories of an aviation tragedy are fresh, the public is more tolerant of the costs and inconveniences associated with changes to safety and security measures.

Table 1
Select Terror Events and Industry Response

Terror Event	Industry Response and Reaction
1968–1972; 326 Skyjacking attempts	Restricted access to aircrew flight station, increased passenger screening, more stringent baggage inspections. Reduced skyjacking attempts from average of 29 attempts per year to 9.3 attempts per year
1988, Pan Am Flight 103 bombing, Lockerbie, Scotland	Reconciliation of checked baggage with passengers, development and use of hardened unit load devices

Table 1
Select Terror Events and Industry Response **(Continued)**

Terror Event	Industry Response and Reaction
September 11, 2001, Terror attacks on World Trade Center and Pentagon, 4 sky-jacked aircraft used as weapons	More stringent passenger screening, limi-tations on acceptable carry-on baggage, hardened cockpit doors preventing unau-thorized access to aircraft
November 2002, surface-to-air missile attack on Israeli airliner, Mombassa, Kenya	Discussions on installing countermeasures capabilities on commercial aircraft

The FAA is the government agency responsible for air safety and the operation of the air traffic control system. The FAA also administers a program that provides grants from the Airport and Airway Trust Fund for airport development. The FAA was established as a federal agency in 1958 to regulate air commerce; it combined the Civil Aeronautics Administration and the Airways Modernization Board. The agency became part of the newly formed Transportation Department in 1967.

The FAA sets standards for the airworthiness of all civilian aircraft, inspects and licenses aircraft, and regulates civilian and military air traffic through its air traffic control centers. It investigates air accidents and, in response, may establish new rules on such issues as de-icing and airframe inspections. It also promotes the development of a national system of airports (FAA, 2001).

What Are the Problems?

According to Joan Claybrook, President of Public Citizen, a National Non-Profit Public Interest Organization states the FAA has been taken over by the very industry it regulates; as a consequence, airline safety and security has become seriously and dangerously lax (Claybrook 2001). Millions of people fly daily for pleasure and employment and depend on airlines—and the FAA's oversight of those airlines—to keep them safe.

The most significant challenges facing the leadership of federal agencies, including the FAA and the aircraft manufacturing and air travel industries, are identifying vulnerabilities in security and implementing preventative measures prior to a successful attack (Wassink 2003; Wassink and Cherry 2003). These challenges are made significantly more complex because market forces drive neither aircraft manufacturers nor the air travel industry toward enhanced safety and security measures. Col. Wassink and I further posit that profitability currently drives the airline industry (Wassink and Cherry 2003). As a result, efforts to enhance safety and security will not be undertaken voluntarily by the aviation industry.

Col. Wassink and I stated in 2003 that federal intervention and direction is required to establish a long-term balance among aviation commerce and profit, aircraft security, and air travel safety. These three forces frequently operate in opposition to one another. Numerous security enhancements, both implemented and proposed, have wide-ranging safety implications.

Joan Claybrook pointed out in 2001 that the lobbying group formed then by the top nine airlines—the Air Transport Association of America, Inc. (ATA)—has spent millions of dollars trying to dissuade the FAA and legislators from passing stronger security measures that would cost the airlines more money. Public Citizen further reported that the Federal Aviation Administration (FAA) should not be permitted to oversee airline and airport security because the agency bows repeatedly to airline industry pressure and has a history of diluting or delaying security-boosting rules after industry complaints.

Public Citizen further suggests and recommends that an aviation law enforcement agency should be created that is either independent of the Department of Transportation and the FAA or is housed at the Department of Justice. Unlike the FAA, this new agency could be devoted exclusively to assessing and addressing aviation security threats and coordinating with other law enforcement agencies.

The ATA represents the major airlines of the world's largest commercial aviation region—North America. Since 1936, the ATA has been providing technical expertise and building specifications for its members and the industry at large. The ATA also provides technical liaison with the U.S. government and has therefore developed a strong relationship with the Federal Aviation Administration and other aeronautical agencies. As a result, the ATA has become a key policy-shaping organization and premier source of information for the U.S. airline industry.

The ATA meets the definition of a *dominant coalition,* a social network of individuals having the greatest influence on the selection of an organization's goals and strategies (Ansoff 1983; Charan 1991; Neilsen and Hayagreeva Rao 1987; Pearce and David 1983; Pearce and DeNisi 1983; Pfeffer and Salancik 1978). In the aviation industry, the top nine airlines—the major stakeholders—have a common interest in preventing the federal government from mandating safety and security changes. The airlines want the safety and security changes, but they insist that the federal government pay for any or all safety and security enhancements.

From 1997 to 2000, according to Joan Claybrook, the ATA spent $62.9 million lobbying the FAA, Congress, and the president

(Claybrook 2001). During that time, according to Claybrook, the government was considering several safety recommendations made by the commission appointed after the crash of TWA Flight 800 off the southern coast of Long Island, New York, in 1996.

According to Claybrook, "In 2000 alone, the airline industry employed 210 lobbyists, including 108 who previously worked for the federal government" (p. 1). The fact that the ATA employed so many former government employees is significant, states Claybrook, because former government employees tend to have more access to members of Congress and therefore wield more influence.

And according to Sheila R. Cherry's 2001 article:

> Since October 30, 2001, more than 100 members of the Office of the Inspector General (OIG) personnel have conducted security observations at 58 airports nationwide. On September 14, 2001, three days after the terrorist attacks, they arrested 12 individuals who were not U.S. citizens who had illegally obtained security badges to gain admittance to secure areas at a major U.S. airport. (p. 1)

Cherry further stated that in October 2001 OIG officials, together with FAA security specialists, were dispatched to scrutinize screening operations at Philadelphia's international airport. In the course of that investigation, they discovered that, despite the airport already being on probation for past violations, "bad practices in the hiring and training of security screeners continued to exist" (p. 1).

Since September 11, 2001, Americans have become all too familiar with the flaws in the nation's aviation security. According to Barry Yeoman and Bill Hogan, "Throughout the 1990s, government inspections designed to intentionally breach airport security met with extraordinary success. Federal inspectors discovered that they could smuggle firearms, hand grenades, and bomb components past screening checkpoints at every airport they visited" (Yeoman and Hogan 2002, 2). In some cases, inspectors got on airplanes with no problems and placed illegal objects throughout the cabins. In one investigation conducted in 1999, "they successfully boarded 117 airplanes, some filled with passengers, and were asked to show identification only one fourth of the time" (Yeoman and Hogan 2002, 2). Mary Schiavo (as cited in Yeoman and Hogan, 2), the inspector general for the Department of Transportation from 1990 to 1996, said that "her office repeatedly recommended security improvements, including a system to match checked bags with onboard passengers." But the FAA wanted no part of this, according to Schiavo. Since there had never been a major incident in the United States, the FAA argued, the risk to passenger safety was too low to warrant any action.

What's the Purpose of This Book?

To examine airline safety and airline security in the post-9/11 society. The premise of the research done was to determine how passengers' perceptions of airline safety and security changed and why they changed.

What Questions Determined My Research?

The overarching question of my research was how passengers' perceptions of airline safety and security have changed since September 11, 2001? This book will address two topical subquestions: what factors have influenced the change in passengers' perceptions, and why have these perceptions changed?

Significance of This Book

This book will help readers more fully understand the impact that 9/11 has had on commercial air travel and how passengers perceive airline safety and security. According to Bernard M. Bass, leadership is regarded as the single most critical factor in the success or failure of institutions (Bass 1990, 8). Lyn Jongbloed and Peter J. Frost (as cited in Bass) argued that leaders would always have an important role. They further argued that leaders manage employees' interpretations and understanding of what goes on in the organization. As stated earlier, I believe that profitability currently drives the airline industry and that airlines will not enact costly safety and security measures voluntarily."

Currently, there is little research in airline safety and security. Several agencies and Web sites study aircraft safety and security, aircraft worthiness, and aircraft accidents, however, there are no formal studies on the impact 9/11 has had on passengers who travel commercial airlines.

2

Historical Review

A Case Study in a Post-9/11 Society

The events of September 11, 2001, the surface-to-air missile attack on an Israeli aircraft in Kenya on November 28, 2002, the crash of Air France A340 on August 3, 2005, and the crash of Northwest 747 on August 27, 2005, have reenergized the safety and security concerns associated with air travel. Although flying is one of the safest forms of transportation, headline-grabbing disasters still occur frequently.

As Col. John Wassink noted, the events of September 11, 2001, dramatically illustrated how terrorists can use commercial aircraft to inflict significant damage and strike fear into the general population (Wassink 2003). From a safety and security perspective, this is not a new challenge because terrorist have always use whatever means necessary to strike fear in people; however, these unprecedented attacks involved a new variation of previously recognized problems associated with skyjacking. Col. Wassink stated that since the early 1970s, passenger-screening procedures have been in use to find people carrying weapons that might be used to take over an aircraft or intimidate the crew into changing the aircraft's destination. The difference between previous skyjacking efforts and the attacks on September 11, 2001, is that, after gaining control of the aircrafts, the attackers used the airplanes as weapons to target infrastructures and not as a bargaining chip to extract some type of concession. Two broad failures allowed these efforts to be successful: the failure of security procedures designed to prevent passengers from seizing control of aircraft and the lack of procedural and technical solutions to prevent unauthorized persons from piloting an aircraft.

To preclude a repeat of the events of September 11, 2001, future efforts in aircraft safety and security must focus on preventing unauthorized control of aircraft.

As there are no empirical studies in this area, in this chapter I will review the history of writings on the state of safety and security in the airline industry. I have grouped the writings into the following categories: the early beginnings of the airline industry, the airline industry at present, and the airline industry as a dominant coalition.

The Airline Industry: The Early Beginnings

> Ferdinand Graf von Zeppelin set up the first commercial airline in 1912, using a form of the dirigible to transport more than 34,000 passengers before World War I. Early air travel began with balloons (first flown by two Frenchmen in 1783), gliders (first flown in 1809), and ultimately airplanes (a Frenchman Clement Ader, flew his steam-powered plane, the Eole, in 1890). (Dooanis and Sampson 2000)

Prior to World War I, "the public's interest in flying was peaked by demonstrations and airplane races; during the war, government subsidies and demands for new airplanes vastly improved techniques for designing and building them" (Dooanis and Sampson). Following the war, the first commercial airplane routes were set up in Europe using wartime pilots and decommissioned warplanes. Passengers were often seated in chairs set up in old bombers. In the 1920s, European governments heavily subsidized the establishment of such well-known commercial airlines as British Airways, Air France, and KLM (Dooanis and Sampson).

In the United States, commercial airlines developed more slowly. The U.S. Post Office established an airmail service in 1919 and played an important role in developing air travel by setting up a nationwide system of airports. In 1925, the U.S. government began paying generous subsidies to private carriers to deliver the mail, and some companies began carrying passengers as well. Many well-known U.S. carriers were established during this period, including Pan Am (created in 1928), United Airlines (created in 1931 by a merger between several older mail-carrying operations), American Airlines (created in 1930 out of several mail carriers), TWA (created in 1928), and Delta (created in 1929) (Dooanis and Sampson 2000).

According to the FAA (2003), the Air Commerce Act of May 20, 1926, was the cornerstone of the federal government's regulation of civil aviation. This landmark legislation was passed at the urging of the aviation industry, whose leaders believed that the airplane could not reach its full commercial potential without federal action to improve and maintain safety standards. The act charged the Secretary of Commerce with fostering air commerce, issuing and enforcing air traffic rules, licensing pilots, certificating aircraft, establishing airways, and operating and maintaining aids to air navigation (FAA 2003). A new aeronautics branch of the Department of Commerce assumed primary responsibility for aviation oversight. The first head of this branch was William P. MacCracken, Jr., who had played a key part in convincing Congress of the need for this new governmental role (FAA 2003).

The imminent introduction of jet airliners and a series of midair collisions hastened passage of the Federal Aviation Act of 1958. This legislation transferred the functions of the Civil Aeronautics Administration (CAA) to a new independent body, the FAA, which was given broader authority to combat aviation hazards. The act removed safety rulemaking from the Civil Aeronautics Board and entrusted it to the new FAA. It also gave the FAA sole responsibility for developing and maintaining a common civil-military system of air navigation and air traffic control, a responsibility that the CAA had shared with others (FAA 2003).

The scope of the Federal Aviation Act owed much to the leadership of Elwood "Pete" Quesada, an Air Force general who had served as President Eisenhower's principle advisor on civil aeronautics. After becoming the first administrator of the agency he had helped to create, Quesada mounted a vigorous campaign for improved airline safety (FAA 2003).

In 1966, Congress authorized the creation of a cabinet department that would combine the major federal transportation responsibilities. This new Department of Transportation began full operations on April 1, 1967. On that day, the agency became one of several modal organizations within the Department of Transportation and received a new name, the Federal Aviation Administration (FAA 2003).

Even before it became part of the Department of Transportation, the FAA had gradually assumed responsibilities not originally envisaged by the Federal Aviation Act. The hijacking epidemic of the 1960s involved the agency in the field of aviation security. In 1968,

Congress vested in the administrator of the FAA the power to pre-scribe aircraft noise standards. The Airport and Airway Develop-ment Act of 1970 placed the agency in charge of a new airport aid program funded by a special aviation trust fund. The same act made the FAA responsible for the safety certification of airports served by air carriers (FAA 2003).

The Airline Industry: The Present

In research published in 2003, I noted that the airline industry is clearly about to undergo great changes, as suggested by the recent shutdown of Vanguard Airlines and the Chapter 11 filings by United Airlines, US Airways, and (just recently) Delta and North-west Airlines (who filed for bankruptcy on September 15, 2005). According to Chris Isidore (Isidore 2005), both Delta and North-west cited the recent spike in jet fuel costs, which have soared nearly 20 percent since June 1, 2005, as the prime reason for seeking pro-tection from creditors under Chapter 11 of federal bankruptcy laws. He further stated the following:

"This is a coincidence, but what a coincidence," said industry consultant Michael Boyd. "This is another 9/11. Most carriers adjusted to that, but now we have another 9/11 that's called fuel. And we have another half of a 9/11 called pensions.

"The problem is there is so much competition out there, that fares get driven into the cellar," he added. "All this does is get two carriers into position where they can better deal with it, but it's not going to solve the basic problem that the industry [pricing] is irra-tional."

Business and commercial travel have declined because of the poor economy. I argue that many travelers are still uneasy about airline safety and security or irritated by the delays and inconvenience of intensified security since 9/11. I also suggest that the FAA has no real solutions to these problems, although technically the FAA does not involve itself with the business aspects of the airlines. The FAA sets rules and guidelines on safety and security for airports and carriers. In addition, I acknowledge that the FAA and the federal government will have to step in and mandate some of these measures. Potential measures could include the following:

1. Enhanced police surveillance at airports

2. Further enhancements and increased vigilance at preboarding screening checkpoints

3. Expanded searches of passengers immediately before boarding

4. A requirement for passengers to provide government-issued photo identification at departure gates

5. Enhanced screening of checked baggage

6. Expanded screening of personnel who access aircraft

7. Enhanced cargo security controls

In my research, I noted that a major issue to emerge from the terrorist attacks has been the poor screening of passengers who had access to the four planes that were used as weapons on September 11, 2001 (Cherry 2003). The present passenger security screening requirements were developed in response to an increase in hijackings prior to 1972. Today, passenger-screening procedures put more emphasis on identifying passengers carrying illegal substances and weapons that could be used to overtake an aircraft and change its destination. Since the events of September 11th, the FAA has been forced to recognize the need to improve security screening and processes at airports. These improvements include, but are not limited to, the following:

a. Enhancing the ability of metal-detection portals to operate effectively

b. Providing better information and a heads up to security screening personnel on the type and location of potential weapons on individuals who trigger metal-detection systems

c. Increasing the detection capabilities of existing systems to detect alloys, plastic explosives, and other materials that may be harmful to passengers or the aircraft

Trace detectors, which react to the vapors or particles of explosives, could be used to detect the presence of explosive materials on passengers or in luggage. These detection procedures could be used to supplement existing metal-detection technologies and build more comprehensive security systems.

In a *New York Times* article in 2001, after the events of 9/11, President Bush stated that the federal government would take on a larger role in airport security and safety. He stated that some airports already met high standards and that his administration would work with state governors to provide visible security measures for those airports that needed help. In this way, the traveling public would know that the federal government was taking airline safety in America seriously.

Grants would be available to airlines to develop stronger cockpit doors and transponders that cannot be switched off from the cockpit. Grants would also be available to pay for video monitors in the cockpit to alert pilots to trouble in the cabin. Other new actions would include arming pilots, increasing the level of air marshals, federalizing the security screening process, and allowing air traffic controllers to land distressed planes by remote access (*New York Times*, September 28, 2001).

According to Robert L. Helmreich, Barbera G. Kanki, and Earl L. Wiener, in response to President Bush's call to strengthen aircraft security, the FAA wrote and published new standards to protect the airplane as well as the cockpit from being taken over and having small-arms fire or explosive devices used against it (Helmreich et al. 2002). The Aviation and Transportation Security Act authorized a mandate that the FAA require operators of more than six thousand airplanes to install reinforced doors by April 9, 2003.

Robert L. Helmreich et al. (2002) further stated that

the doors will be designed to resist intrusion by a person who attempts to enter using physical force. This includes the door, its means of attachment to the surrounding structure, and the attachment structure on the bulkhead itself. The doors will be designed to resist intrusion by a person who attempts to enter using physical force. The door also will be designed to prevent passengers from opening it without the pilot's permission. An internal locking device will be designed so that it can only be unlocked from inside the cockpit. The purchase and installation cost of an enhanced cockpit door is estimated at between $12,000 and $17,000. Funding will be provided through grants or cost sharing arrangements. The President requested $300 million from Congress to help fund these initiatives. Congress appropriated $100 million.

The article reported that U.S. Transportation Secretary Norman Y. Mineta said, "...fortifying cockpit doors is a critical part of assuring the safety and security of our aviation system."

Mr. Mineta (as cited in Helmreich et al. 2002) went on to say that the September 11, 2001, use of commercial airliners as weapons of mass destruction had ensured that major changes would be made in airport security, going beyond such measures as the elimination of curbside baggage check-in. Measures to counter these problems would include transferring airport security to a not-for-profit corporation or imposing strict federal standards on the private firms currently performing the task. There is widespread support among business travelers for federalizing airport security, according to surveys conducted by the National Business Travel Association (Helmreich et al.).

According to Col. Wassink, safety and security measures must focus on preventing external weapons from being employed against or being introduced into the aircraft, in addition to minimizing damage and destruction if such an attack proved successful (Wassink 2003). Future air travel will remain reliant on electronic aids to navigation, including both ground-based systems and global-positioning systems. Col. Wassink also stated that aircraft flight control systems will become more reliant on electronic programming and automatic operations to improve efficiency and reduce aircrew workload.

Robert W. Hahn wrote in 1997:

> Each measure to improve safety and security can increase the direct costs to travelers, cause delays and inconvenience, infringe on civil liberties, increase taxpayer costs, and even increase fatalities. For example, using high-tech machines may detect some

explosives in checked luggage, but the devices are costly and far from foolproof. Requiring airlines to match each bag to a passenger may reduce the threat of a drop-and-run terrorist tactic, but it could cause lengthy delays and inconvenience. (p. 792)

Hahn further stated that

using computer background checks to identify suspected terrorists could enhance security at a reasonable cost, but it would also curtail individual freedoms. Mandating child safety seats would secure infants during air travel, but the higher costs could lead to an increase in automobile travel and highway fatalities. (p. 792)

Hahn also suggested that "improving air safety and security are important, but we need to assess the cost and effectiveness of each measure before we spend billions of taxpayers' and travelers' money on safety and security measures" (p. 793). Moreover, Alan Levin acknowledged that "we need to confront the question of how safe is safe enough. The sad truth is that aviation fatalities cannot be eliminated unless we ban air travel, and that is simply too high a price to pay" (p. 793).

Another potential measure is arming pilots with weapons. There are views on both sides of this issue. A proposal to make airline pilots eligible to carry guns passed the House of Representatives in July 2002 and the Senate in September 2002 (Levin 2002). "Groups such as the National Rifle Association urged lawmakers to vote for the measure, and few wanted to oppose it in an election year" (Levin 2002, 2). Levin stated that the Bush administration initially opposed arming pilots, but that position weakened under intense lobbying. James Loy, the acting head of the Transportation Security Administration, says he will follow Congress' wishes, though he would prefer to begin with a small test program instead of allowing all pilots to participate. (Levin 2002, 2)

Prevention versus Protection

Two broad options exist for defining safety and security measures. Col. Wassink and I found that these measures can be designed to prevent an attack against the aircraft, aircrew, and passengers, or they can be designed to protect the aircraft, aircrew, and passengers by minimizing the effects of such an attack (Wassink and Cherry 2003). We also pointed out that enhanced safety and security result from an appropriate combination of preventive and protective measures.

One significant challenge is to find the most cost-effective balance among multiple safety and security options. This choice involves substantial difficulties because the implementation of any measure will have both direct and indirect costs. Indirect costs, such as the impact that increased security delays might have on travel demand, can only be estimated. Conversely, increased security, even with slightly longer delays, might boost traveler confidence and ultimately increase revenue and profit. An additional challenge arises from the need to analyze the potential consequences of implementing preventive and protective measures to ensure that they do not lead to decreased air-travel safety or present or create additional vulnerabilities that might be exploited by malicious persons.

Col. Wassink and I considered that the primary purpose of preventive measures is to deny malicious individuals the ability to bring

weapons onto an aircraft. Generally, these persons want to intro-
duce weapons into an aircraft for one of two reasons: the weapons
are designed to destroy the aircraft and its passengers or the weapons
can be used to take over the aircraft or intimidate the aircrew.
Examples of preventive measures include controlling aircraft access,
screening passengers, and matching baggage to passengers. Additional examples include widening the airport security perimeter and
protecting aircraft control and navigation systems.

Col. Wassink and I also considered that the primary purpose of
protective measures is to ensure that the failure of any preventive
measures does not allow weapons to be introduced into the aircraft.
Protective measures should seek to reduce aircraft damage, limit
bodily harm to passengers, and preclude the airplane from being
flown to a location other than its original destination either by the
aircrew under duress or by malicious persons. Examples of protective measures include hardened cockpit doors, arming pilots,
increased use of sky marshals, and video monitoring systems.

"There's so many unknowns," says Dave Barger, President of Jet-
Blue Airlines (as cited in Levin 2002, 3). "I don't think the legislation has really been thought out" (p. 3). Aviation safety advocates
say giving pilots the added responsibility for security could threaten
safety by disrupting their normal routines. "We've trained these
pilots so carefully, and we've ingrained in them that predictable routine makes it safe," says Susan Coughlin, a former member of the
National Transportation Safety Board and president of the Aviation
Safety Alliance. "Let's let them do that and let law enforcement do
the rest" (as cited in Levin 2002, 3).

There is also the cost factor. I previously estimated that such measures would impose costs on either the airlines or the administra-

tion. The bottom line is that someone will eventually have to pay. Current estimates of the costs vary. James Loy (as cited in Levin 2002) projected up to $900 million in initial costs, followed by $250 million per year. "The Air Line Pilots Association, the nation's largest pilots union and a proponent of arming flight crews, estimated it would cost no more than $100 million initially, and probably far less" (Levin 2002, 3).

With safety and security being just two of the many serious problems threatening the entire airline industry, analysts believe that the industry's dominant players have aligned themselves as a dominant coalition to better face these problems.

The Airline Industry: A Dominant Coalition

As stated earlier, the ATA has spent millions of dollars trying to dissuade the FAA and legislators from passing stronger security measures that would cost the airlines more money (Public Citizen Report 2002). The ATA fits the definition of a dominant coalition, a social network of individuals having the greatest influence on the selection of an organization's goals and strategies (Ansoff 1983; Charan 1991; Neilsen and Hayagreeva Rao 1987; Pearce and David 1983; Pearce and DeNisi 1983; Pfeffer and Salancik 1978). A dominant coalition is held together by the members' recognition of some common interests (Pfeffer 1981) and by explicit or implicit agreements about the type of behavior that should be followed (Pennings 1981; Pondy and Mitroff 1979). The major stakeholders—the top nine airlines—have a common interest in trying to keep the federal government from mandating safety and security changes. The airline industry and its leaders are cognizant of the changes that need to be made, but insists these changes should come at the expense of the federal government.

The concept of a dominant coalition is useful because it grants that both individuals and groups have influence (though not equally) over organizational actions (Scott 1967). Some conflicting interests can be resolved through negotiation; some cannot. In most cases, the dominant coalition also changes over time (Scott). Since its inception in 1936, the ATA continues to play a major role in all major government decisions regarding aviation, including the creation of the Civil Aeronautics Board, the creation of the air traffic control system, airline deregulation, and most recently in dealing with the aftermath of the 9/11 attack on America.

According to the ATA, the fundamental purpose of the association is to foster a business environment that will permit U.S. airlines to flourish. By working with members in the technical, legal, and political arenas, the ATA supports measures that enhance aviation safety, airline security, and industry well-being. The ATA and its members continue to play a vital role in shaping the future of air transportation.

Power and money are two of the key variables that significantly impact the airline industry and the outcome of certain key decisions. Power and money are independent variables, but they are also dependent upon each other. With one, you will always have the other.

Top Management Teams

According to Hambrick and Mason (1984), the term *dominant coalition* is used often alongside the term *top management team* (TMT). The members of a TMT can be simply identified as those executives at the top of the firm's organization chart (Hambrick & Mason). Their aspirations, orientations, and behaviors are assumed to be identical to those described for a dominant coalition (Priem 1990). Often, these assumptions are accurate; even more frequently, perhaps, they are *almost* accurate (Priem). Serious conflicts can arise when the two groups do not completely overlap—when members of the TMT are not members of the dominant coalition (Pearce 1995). For example, when a highly positioned executive is excluded from participation in strategy formulation or when a person not easily identified as a TMT member wields considerable influence over the nominal leaders of the organization, subordinate managers are likely to perceive mixed signals about the implications of strategic decisions that are announced (Pearce).

Summary of the Historical Review

According to the FAA (2003), the Air Commerce Act of May 20, 1926, was the cornerstone of the federal government's regulation of civil aviation. As we look back, the scope of the Federal Aviation Act owed much to the leadership of Elwood "Pete" Quesada, an Air Force general who had served as President Eisenhower's principle advisor on civil aeronautics. After becoming the first administrator of the agency he had helped to create, Quesada mounted a vigorous campaign for improved airline safety (FAA 2003).

It was not until 1966 that Congress authorized the creation of a cabinet department that would combine the major federal transportation responsibilities. This new Department of Transportation began full operations on April 1, 1967. On that day, the agency became one of several modal organizations within the Department of Transportation and received a new name, the Federal Aviation Administration (FAA 2003).

After the events of 9/11, President Bush stated that the federal government would take on a larger role in airport security and safety. He stated that some airports already met high standards and that his administration would work with state governors to provide visible security measures for those airports that needed help. In this way, the traveling public would know that the federal government was taking airline safety in America seriously. He also stated that grants would be available to airlines to develop stronger cockpit doors and transponders that cannot be switched off from the cockpit. Grants would also be available to pay for video monitors in the cockpit to alert pilots to trouble in the cabin. Other new actions would include arming pilots, increasing the level of air marshals, federalizing the security screening process, and allowing air traffic controllers to land distressed planes by remote access (*New York Times*, September 28, 2001).

The ATA has spent millions of dollars trying to disuade legislators from passing stronger security measures that would cost the airlines more money (Public Citizen Report 2002). The ATA fits the definition of a dominant coalition, a social network of individuals having the greatest influence on the selection of an organization's goals and strategies (Ansoff 1983; Charan 1991; Neilsen and Hayagreeva Rao 1987; Pearce and David 1983; Pearce and DeNisi 1983; Pfeffer and Salancik 1978). The concept of a dominant coalition is useful because it grants that both individuals and groups have influence (though not equally) over organizational actions (Scott

1967). In most cases, the dominant coalition also changes over time (Scott). Since its inception in 1936, the ATA continues to play a major role in all major government decisions regarding aviation, including the creation of the Civil Aeronautics Board, the creation of the air traffic control system, airline deregulation, and most recently in dealing with the aftermath of the 9/11 attack on America.

3

I Approached the Problem

Overview

In order to get an accurate sense of current perceptions of airline safety and security, I had to investigate the topic formally. I sought to examine airline safety and airline security in post-9/11 society. As stated earlier, I was not primarily concerned with the attitudes and mind-sets of passengers after September 11, 2001.

I sought to address the following questions:

- How have the perceptions of passengers changed since September 11, 2001, in regard to airline safety and airline security?

- What factors have influenced the change in passengers' perceptions?

- Why have these perceptions changed?

Context of the Study

To gain greater insight into professional attitudes about airline safety and security, I interviewed employees of the National Defense University (NDU), SAS Inc., The Whitlock Group, and coworkers and subordinates. It was my intention to interview a representation of all types of people. Over five hundred personnel of diverse nationalities and backgrounds attend the two senior service schools at the National Defense University. I received permission from the Industrial College of the Armed Forces to interview members of the Aircraft Industry Study. (Sixteen members were assigned to this study.) I also interviewed other service members, Department of Defense civilians, and non-Department of Defense personnel. I have a considerable understanding of this industry, as I was a member of the study during my academic year at the college.

My Role as the Researcher

I recently completed a year of study at Industrial College of the Armed Forces, National Defense University in Washington DC. During my second semester, I was a member of the Aircraft Industry Study. I also partnered with a fellow student to conduct an extensive research study for the FAA. The FAA commissioned the Industrial College of the Armed Forces to conduct research to identify and analyze functional and operational relationships between aircraft safety and aircraft security. This research involved discussions with major aircraft and aircraft engine manufacturers in the United States, the United Kingdom, and Sweden; extensive travel through national and international airports; and comprehensive library study of potential threats, current airport security procedures, technologies available to enhance aircraft safety and security, and additional security measures initiated following the events of September 11, 2001.

Discussions during the domestic and international travel phases of this study provided insight into current industry perspectives on safety and security issues, market forces impacting efforts to enhance aircraft safety and security, and factors affecting the current and future health of the aircraft industry. Our final report is on file with the FAA and the National Defense University. During my dissertation, my committee chair approved the overall research design as well as major changes to the research design. In addition, my committee chair and two university professors guided, advised, and directed my entire dissertation process. This oversight increased the likelihood that any errors compromising this study's design would be discovered before they were implemented.

Collecting the Answers

For this study, I used standardized, open-ended interviews, documentation review, and observations. I collected and organized my findings to develop grounded theory from the situation as well as to provide an audit trail for those who might want to investigate this topic after me.

Background on the Interviews

Each individual was contacted and consented to the interview. During the contact, I introduced myself and explained to them the purpose of my research. One hundred percent of the people I contacted agreed to be interviewed. Each person interviewed was given the Airline Safety and Security Interview (see the end of this chapter) and the Participant Consent Form. For reasons of distance or convenience, four participants completed the interview via e-mail.

I targeted the members of the Aircraft Industry Study at the Industrial College of the Armed Forces to complete the Airline Safety and Airline Security Interview. There are sixteen members assigned to this study. I also interviewed other service members,

Department of Defense civilians, and non-Department of Defense personnel. There was one protocol for all interviewees.

The first part of the questionnaire, consisting of seven open-ended questions, targeted demographics. During my studies at the Industrial College of the Armed Forces and as a member of the Aircraft Industry Study Seminar, I engaged in various discussions with top members of the airline industry and traveled to their domestic and international headquarters.

In the course of this research, I formulated a series of questions that were not being addressed by the industry. Issues and topics such as turbulence, midair collisions, and bombings were being addressed, but there were no surveys or studies regarding how passengers' perceptions have changed in regard to airline safety and security, what the factors have influenced this change, or why this change has occurred in post-9/11 society. This questionnaire addressed those issues and concerns.

The interview consisted of the following questions:

1. Since September 11, 2001, how has your perception changed in regard to airline safety and airline security? Explain.

2. In what areas has this change taken place? Explain.

3. What factors have influenced this perception change? Explain.

4. How did you feel before the 9/11 attack, immediately after the attack, and now? Explain.

5. Do you feel that the FAA (Federal Aviation Administration) and the Federal government are doing enough in the areas of airline safety and security? Explain.

6. Do you feel safe when you travel on airplanes? Explain.

7. What are your thoughts and fears? Any other additional feed-back you wish to add?

These questions are not exclusive to this research but help us understand the mindsets of individuals who travel on airplanes. During this six-month study, I learned a lot about the undertakings of this industry. The most helpful tool I used to better understand this industry was AirSafe.com. AirSafe.com is a free e-mail newsletter that provides insights into critical issues in aviation safety and security. Since it began, AirSafe.com has sought to provide the aviation safety community and the general public with factual and timely information about events that involve the airline industry. AirSafe.com also provides fatal-event information by airline and by aircraft model and information about current aviation safety issues. In addition to airline safety, AirSafe.com provides a range of information and resources including information on the fear of flying, lists of aviation-related books, and links to numerous travel and travel-safety sites.

Background on the Focus Study Group

I conducted a focus-study group on March 2, 2004, at the SAS Institute in Arlington, Virginia. Five individuals participated in the study and are identified as Research Participants 1 through 5. SAS is the world's largest privately held software company and has head-quarters in Cary, North Carolina.

According to Susan Dawson and Lenore Manderson, focus groups consist of five to eight people gathered to discuss a topic of interest. The discussion is guided by a group leader, moderator, or—in the case of this study—a researcher who asks questions and tries to help the group have a natural and free conversation. Focus groups are aimed at encouraging participants to talk with each other rather than answer questions directly to the moderator. The interaction between members of focus groups is important because it gives us some understanding of how the participants are thinking about the topic.

I asked the same questions during the focus group that I asked during the individual interviews. Again, the focus was on airline safety and airline security in a post-9/11 society. Follow-up questions were asked of the group during the study. These questions were based on the dialogue that was going back and forth between the participants of the study. The questions asked were related to the conduct and outcome of the study.

What Relationship Did I Study?

The premise for this book is to examine how the perceptions of passengers have changed since September 11, 2001, in regard to airline safety and airline security, what factors have influenced the change in passengers' perceptions, and why these perceptions have changed.

Why Should We Study This Relationship?

Since 9/11, airline safety and airline security have consistently been topics of interest domestically and internationally. Col. John Wassink and I suggested that September 11, 2001, dramatically illustrated the potential for terrorists to use commercial aircraft to inflict significant economic and infrastructural damage and strike fear into the general population. Unfortunately, from a safety and security perspective, this was not a new challenge to be countered. As previously mentioned, Col. Wassink and I noted that since the early 1970s, passenger-screening procedures have been in use to find passengers carrying weapons that might be used to take over an aircraft or intimidate the crew into changing its destination.

In Summary

For this book, I examined the relationship between airline safety and airline security in a post-9/11 society. According to Col. Wassink, the significant economic impact caused by the events of September 11, 2001, clearly illustrates a requirement to better anticipate potential threats and to design solutions before a terrorist event can exploit unanticipated vulnerabilities. Col. Wassink further suggested that the U.S. aircraft manufacturing industry would be hard-pressed to absorb the aircraft-demand downfall associated with another devastating aircraft terrorist event. Economic pressures from potential threats will not provide sufficient justification for aircraft manufacturers to devote the resources necessary to design technical solutions to future vulnerabilities.

My research adds to the nonexistent body of knowledge in the area of airline safety and airline security by seeking to determine how the perceptions of passengers have changed since September 11, 2001, what factors have influenced the change in passengers' perceptions, and why these perceptions have changed.

AIRLINE SAFETY AND SECURITY INTERVIEW

You are being asked to participate in an important interview. The purpose of this interview is to understand airline safety and airline security in a post-9/11 society and to determine how airline safety and airline security have changed in the perception of passengers and why. This survey is designed to be useful for both the airline and private industry. Please make every effort to respond to each question. The interview is divided into two separate parts: a demographic section and the interview itself. There are a total of seven questions in this interview. Following the demographic questions, please respond to the following questions of this interview.

Demographic Questions

Please place an X by the appropriate response.

A. **What is your gender?**

____ Male

____ Female

B. **What is your age? (Range)**

____ 20 to 30

____ 31 to 40

____ 41 to 50

____ 51 to 60

____ 61 and up

C. **What is your marital status?**

____ Married

____ Divorced/separated

___ Single (never been married)
___ Widowed
___ Domestic Partner

D. What was the last year of school completed?

___ Some high school	___ College graduate
___ High school graduate	___ Some post-graduate work
___ Some College	___ Post-graduate degree

E. Are you?

___ Caucasian/White
___ Asian (Chinese, Japanese)
___ Black (African-American, Caribbean)
___ Native American
___ Hispanic (Latin-American, Mexican)
___ Other (Specify) _____

F. What is your current occupation?

___ Proprietor/Business Owner
___ Executive/Administrator
___ Manager (All Levels)
___ Professional Specialty (e.g., Doctor, Lawyer,
Scientist, Teacher)
___ Professional Technician (e.g., Paralegal, Dental
Hygienist)
___ Service (e.g., Police, Fireman, Chef, Flight
Attendant, Commercial Pilot)
___ Armed Forces (To include the Coast Guard)
___ Administrative and Clerical Support

____ Retired

G. How often do you travel on airplanes?
____ Never
____ Daily
____ Weekly
____ Monthly
____ Quarterly
____ Semi-annually
____ Annually

AIRLINE SAFETY AND SECURITY INTERVIEW

Operational Definitions

Air safety is concerned with the rules for the construction and use of aircraft.
Airline security is aimed at the prevention of illegal acts in the field of aviation.

1. Since September 11, 2001, (9/11) how has your perception changed in regard to airline safety and airline security? Explain.

2. In what areas have this change taken place? Explain

3. What factors have influenced this perception change? Explain

4. How did you feel before the attack, immediately after the attack and now? Explain

5. Do you feel that the FAA (Federal Aviation Administration) and the federal government are doing enough in the areas of airline safety and security? Explain.

6. Do you feel safe when you travel on airplanes? Explain.

7. What are your thoughts and fears? Is there any other additional feedback you wish to add?

4

What I Learned, And What You Should Know

Introduction

Two of the most important issues facing this nation and world today are airline safety and security. As a recent study conducted by Col. John Wassink and myself showed, major increases in safety and security efforts are implemented consistently in response to successful terror attacks.

My research for this book examined airline safety and airline security in our post-9/11 society. The premise of this research endeavor was to determine how passengers' perceptions of airline safety and airline security had changed, what factors had led to the change in perception, and why this change had occurred. As previously defined, airline safety is concerned with the rules for the construction and use of aircraft, and airline security is aimed at the prevention of illegal acts in the field of aviation.

What Are the Current Problems?

According to Joan Claybrook, the FAA has been taken over by the very industry it regulates; as a consequence, airline safety and security have become seriously and dangerously lax. She further stated that millions of people fly daily for pleasure and employment and depend on airlines—and the FAA's oversight of those airlines—to keep them safe.

Col. Wassink and I considered the most significant challenges for the leadership of these federal agencies (including the FAA and the aircraft manufacturing and air travel industries) to be identifying vulnerabilities and implementing a combination of technical and procedural solutions prior to a successful attack. According to John A. Anderson and Stephen D. Fulton these include the following:

1. The preprogrammed nature of RNP (Required Navigation Program) enables flight-path information to be loaded such that the system will automatically avoid overflight of areas with high strategic importance or critical infrastructure.

2. The system can be enhanced to provide immediate indications to ground-control facilities when an aircraft strays from its preprogrammed path of flight without any overt communications from the aircraft's flight crew.

3. The potential also exists to allow aircraft control to be locked in based on coded permission from the flight crew. In this situation, the aircraft flight path could not be diverted or reprogrammed.

These challenges are made significantly more complex because market forces (profits) drive neither aircraft manufacturers nor the air travel industry toward enhanced safety and security measures. For this reason, efforts to enhance safety and security will not be taken voluntarily by the aviation industry.

Review of the Research and Demographics

My study was conducted from a naturalistic inquiry approach in the form of a case study. According to the Writing Center at Colorado State University (2003), a case study is the collection and presentation of detailed information about a particular participant or small group frequently including the accounts of subjects themselves. A form of qualitative descriptive research, the case study looks intensely at an individual or small participant pool, drawing conclusions only about that participant or group and only in that specific context.

I asked twenty-one people to complete an initial interview. All twenty-one completed the survey, and all were usable. The group consisted of fifteen males (71 percent) and six females (29 percent). There were eleven participants (52 percent) with postgraduate degrees, five college graduates (24 percent) with some postgraduate work completed, and five college graduates (24 percent). Table 2 breaks down the demographics of all respondents to include frequency of travel.

Table 2
Demographic Data and Percentages

Sample	F (*N*= 21)	P

Table 2
Demographic Data and Percentages (Continued)

Gender	Male	16	71%
	Female	5	29%
Ethnicity/Race	Caucasian	14	66%
	African American	4	19%
	Hispanic	1	5%
	Other (Finnish)	1	5%
	Other (Polish)	1	5%
Age	31–40 years	1	5%
	41–50 years	12	57%
	51–60 years	7	33%
	61 years and over	1	5%
Education	College Graduate	5	24%
	Some Postgraduate Work	5	24%
	Postgraduate Degree	11	52%
Travel	Never	1	5%
	Monthly	10	47%
	Quarterly	8	38%
	Semiannually	1	5%
	Annually	1	5%

Lessons from My Discussions

During the course of the interviews and focus study group, there was much discussion in all the areas I identified in regard to airline safety and airline security. Also, the participants emphasized a constant theme throughout this process—leadership. As mentioned previously, Bernard M. Bass cites leadership as the single most critical factor in the success or failure of institutions. And Lyn Jongbloed and Peter J. Frost (as cited in Bass) argue that leaders would always have an important role. They further argue that leaders manage employees' interpretations and understanding of what is going on in the organization. They further posit that their leadership exerts a strong impact on organizational outcomes.

How Have Passengers' Perceptions Changed Since 9/11 Regarding Airline Safety and Security?

In the area of perception changes, there were two schools of thought. First and foremost, respondents were shocked that individuals would use an airplane as a weapon to create havoc and destroy the lives of innocent people. As one interviewee said, "No one could have ever imagined using a plane as a weapon of mass destruction." Another noted, "Pre-September 11th, I never felt threatened or thought about terrorism through the use of airplanes. Other than the chance of a hijacking, which I thought would probably happen in a foreign country, the thought never occurred to me that this type of violence would happen in America."

Some respondents felt that the increased security measures made them feel safe as they traveled through airports. One said, "It appears more measures have been taken by the government and the airlines to build a sense of security among airline travelers." Seeing more security, military personnel, and the addition of sky marshals on flights has given them an added sense of security. "More security measures, for example, screening of passengers, luggage/packages, identification checks, removal of certain carry-on items, on-board marshals, training for airline personnel, et cetera, seem to be in place now," said one respondent. Another noted the changes in procedure that increased the perception of safety such as "visible evidence of more airport security, only those boarding allowed in the airport terminals, vehicles not allowed to drive in certain areas near terminals, and extended amounts of time needed prior to checking in with the chosen airline."

Also, most travelers stated they were more aware of their surroundings and had a watchful eye. One flier, noticing more than in the past, said, "I think about who my fellow passengers are and scan the first class when I board." Another suggested, "I find that I am much more alert to the airport environment, cautious to the movements and actions of other travelers. I suppose I consider that to be my contribution—to assist in identifying any potential perpetrators. It is easy to sense the tension amongst others and even their suspicions of you as you take off your shoes, unbuckle your belt, and reveal yourself at the security gate."

The second school of thought was that not enough was being done in the areas of airline safety and airline security. As one interviewee pessimistically suggested, "I don't think there will ever be enough done to guarantee complete safety and security for any industry. For every effort that is being made to ensure safety, there is probably someone trying to figure out a way to overcome it."

Some believed we have had a "knee-jerk reaction" in the form of the addition of baggage handlers and inspections. As one flier noted, "Adding more personnel will not stop a terrorist." Another respondent noted, "The addition of more baggage personnel is not the answer. Seeing military guards at the entrance to gates also would not deter a terrorist. They would definitely find a way to work around this obstacle, if not have one of their own in the position to inspect the bag. Only an idiot would cause a problem at that point."

Recent breaches in security in airports have only made travelers more uncomfortable:

- "My perception is still uncertainty in terms of safety due to recent breach of security three times by a college student. I still believe the airlines are no safer than before 9/11."

- "Too many cases exist of security breaches. Improvements have been made in baggage and passenger screening systems, but I'm not sure that baggage handlers get the same scrutiny."

- "The college student was able to breach security and prove a point of unsafe and unreliable security and safety measures. Yet the FAA has arrested this individual for disclosing their broken system of lax security."

Some respondents felt that there had been a lot of "fluff" to make people feel good about flying:

"They're trying to implement a lot of things to make people feel good about flying. There are certain things that are good. But taking off your shoes or detaining the eighty-five-year-old grandmother with the fingernail file is not the answer. They've got the eighty-five-year-old terrorist grandmothers under control. In my perception, they have done things to make us feel better, but they are not necessarily the things that will do better."

Another flier provided equally stinging criticism:

"You see a lot more security at the airport itself. A lot of this is also being done to calm society and calm the general public [by showing] that drastic measures are being [taken]. You still see the security guards sleeping at stations. You still see x-ray people chatting and not paying attention. They try and give you a warm and fuzzy feeling, and they are not doing it as a serious undertaking or taking the security and safety seriously. You see guards falling asleep. I think, to a certain degree, it's window dressing. After 9/11, you saw the National Guardsmen out there with M-16s and fully loaded for combat. Now you see a couple guys with a security badge on who may or may not speak English. Security has dropped a couple notches."

The extra delays in checking in and being constantly searched have added to passenger frustration and attitudes. As one flier said when it comes to driving to the airport, "A faster means to get to your destination is no longer the case if it is a short distance when you take into account the pre-[departure] time."

According to Steve Booth-Butterfield, people need consistency in their lives. The bottom line is things must work together and make sense. When they do not, we have a problem that we must solve. Consistency theory was proposed to explain what happens when things happen in inconsistent and unexpected ways.

Booth-Butterfield's 1988 theory is divided into three steps:

1. People expect consistency

2. Inconsistencies create a state of dissonance

3. Dissonance drives us to restore consistency

Currently, we, the citizens of the United States, are at Step 2, a state of dissonance. According to Booth-Butterfield, consistency is very important and, as much as we need it, there are times when things happen in unexpected ways. There is an inconsistency between what we expect and what we receive.

On September 11, 2001, terrorists gained control of four commercial aircraft in order to inflict significant economic and infra-structural damage as well as strike fear in the general population.

This was a new variation on previously recognized problems associated with skyjacking. The difference between previous skyjack efforts and the events of September 11, 2001, was that after gaining control of the aircraft the attackers used it as a weapon to target infrastructures and not as a bargaining chip to extract some type of concession from the government.

The state that arises following inconsistency is called *dissonance*. Dissonance is simply a technical term for the cognitive, emotional, physiological, and behavioral state that arises when things do not go the way we expect them. Today we are still in a state of dissonance. Based on the interviews and focus study group I conducted, I can conclude that the perception exists that our security measures are not standardized within the United States and certainly not outside our borders. As one flier notes, there is a thirty-minute seating policy when you fly out of Washington DC but not elsewhere. Also, since 9/11, travelers' perceptions of airline safety and airline security are divided. Some passengers will continue to travel by air because they still believe it is the safest mode of travel, and there are others who flew before but will never fly again due to the events that took place on 9/11. Some of their views include the following:

"I prefer not to fly out of Los Angeles, and [I] use smaller airports when possible."

"I used to fly to New York for the weekend—no more. I only travel to see family or on business."

"My perception is that more needs to be done, and I am one hundred percent for adding locked cockpits and steel doors to the cockpits and an air marshal to the flights. And [I] don't object to the increased cost of the ticket for doing this."

"My perception is still uncertain in terms of safety."

"My perception is we are at the beginning of succeeding at this process because good security is a system of systems."

"The airlines and airports have beefed up their security efforts. Overall, I feel more secure while traveling via air transportation."

Leaders have the responsibility to assess their organizations and to attain an understanding of any problems or potential problems in order to find solutions. According to Max DePree, the first responsibility of a leader is to define reality. Leaders have to get a sense of their organizations and determine what turns on and off their personnel. For the airline industry, this means understanding the perceptions of passengers when it comes to safety and security. Some examples include the following:

Respondents were shocked that individuals would use an airplane as a weapon to create havoc and destroy the lives of innocent people.

Some respondents said that the increased security measures made them feel safe as they traveled through airports. The presence of more security and military personnel and the addition of sky marshals on flights have given them an added sense of security.

Some people do not think there can ever be enough done to guarantee complete safety and security in any industry. For every effort that is being made to ensure safety, there is probably someone trying to figure out a way to overcome it.

One respondent noted that adding more personnel would not stop a terrorist.

Also, most travelers stated they were more aware of their surroundings and had a watchful eye.

Now, the federal government, the FAA, and their supporting agencies have to address the problem of reality versus passenger perception. Booth-Butterfield claimed that we have a strong preference for consistency in our lives. We want things to work the same way every time they happen. When we wake up in the morning, we want to find the floor under our feet, the sun above our heads, and coffee in our cups. And just as we expect these kinds of physical consistencies, we also expect psychological consistency. If we had marriages, families, and jobs yesterday, then we expect to find them today in pretty much the same condition as yesterday. There was inconsistency between what we expected in our world and what actually occurred on September 11, 2001. On this day, terrorists gained control of four commercial aircraft and inflicted significant economic and infrastructure damage and struck fear into the general population. This was a new variation on previously recognized problems associated with skyjacking.

In regard to airline safety and airline security, travelers expect consistency among airports, no matter how small or how large. This is paramount in leadership: leaders assess their organizations, identify problems, and find solutions to the problems.

What Factors Have Influenced the Change in Passengers' Perceptions?

I sought to determine the factors that have caused passenger perceptions to change since 9/11. Some fliers readily detect factors that represent progress in airline safety and security:

- "Visible evidence of more airport security, such as [the fact that] only those boarding are allowed in the airport terminals."

- "I have been to various airports, and they all seem to have the same protocol for securing the airport facility."

- "Physical changes to the aircraft, such as [installing a] door to [the] cockpit. Addition of air marshals traveling on aircraft. Increased security checks of person's luggage prior to boarding. Greater media coverage of events that may delay or cancel flights—possible threats. FAA directives that mandate changes."

Others perceive factors that only make them feel less secure about air travel:

- "Very lax immigration policies, systems, and a very lax Immigration Naturalization Services organization."

- "Two coworkers and I were standing in a room right over there and saw the plane hit the Pentagon. That definitely influenced my perception of airline safety. Seeing the Twin Towers fall every three minutes for the last three years on TV has influenced it.

- "Influence is your perception because you are bombarded every day or almost every day with some yahoo who gets on television and says, 'I'm going to do the next Twin Towers, and I will make it look like nothing.'"

Why Have These Perceptions Changed?

The final question I addressed during this research was, "Why have passenger perceptions changed?" The attacks on the World Trade Center and the Pentagon caused people to question a number of things they had always believed about safety and security. We continue to ask the why question because we do not have all the answers and because not knowing all the answers adds stress to our lives.

A terrorist attack is not the same as a natural disaster, where we often have some advance warning as to what is about to happen. For example, before Hurricanes Katrina and Rita made landfall, many lives were saved (though, sadly, not enough) because of advance orders to evacuate the Gulf Coast. According to the Red Cross, disasters caused by human beings can be more frightening than natural disasters such as floods and hurricanes for the following reasons.

1. There is no warning and no time to get ready. Unlike a hurricane or slow-rising flood, we have no way to prepare ourselves mentally for this kind of disaster.

2. We do not expect this kind of disaster. Most of the disasters in this country are either weather related or accidental. We have almost no history of major terrorist attacks and find it difficult to believe that one could happen.

3. It is hard to understand why anybody would deliberately do something that would cause death and injury, especially when children are involved.

4. Television, radio, and newspaper coverage can make us all feel like part of the disaster, and they make each of us a "victim" of the disaster because we become so concerned.

5. There are no guarantees that a terrorist attack could not happen anywhere. Experts are looking at ways to prevent major terrorist attacks from happening without taking away our freedoms.

Although we cannot always prepare for these types of events or disasters, we must remain vigilant, always focused, and aware of our surroundings.

During the individual interviews and the focus study group, I asked two additional questions that produced interesting results. I asked, how did you feel before the attack, immediately after the attack, and now?" I learned from my research participants that people before the attack were in a routine; they went to the airport, got on the plane, flew, and never worried about security. This seemed normal, even despite some may or may not knew the risks of flying. One interviewee noted, "Before the attack, I felt safe from terrorists. I was more worried about mechanical failure than security breaches. But years ago, we had tons of hijackings all over the world and bombings."

After the 9/11 attacks, people became more cautious and more afraid to fly. People who continued to fly were more cautious of their surroundings. They did not mind the delays, going to the airport two hours early, or the intense security screenings. The same interviewee quoted in the previous paragraph also said, "Immediately after the attack, I felt safe. I didn't think the terrorists would try it again so soon." Many others have echoed her sentiments.

Now, I believe everything is going back to the status quo. People do not want to be delayed, to arrive two hours early, and to constantly go through security-screening checkpoints. They do not want to remove some articles of clothing like their jacket, shoes, and belt and be asked a lot of questions. They want to arrive at the airport, check in, go to their plane, and fly to their destination. I call this the "hassle factor." People are tired of the delays, do not want to go through checkpoint after checkpoint, do not want to be asked the same question five or six times, and do not want to be stripped and searched. When asked about their feelings before and after 9/11, respondents offered some of the following comments:

- "[I felt] safe before 9/11. [I was] angry after the attack and [wanted] to punish the responsible individuals, organizations, or nations."

- "Pre-September 11, I never felt threatened or thought about terrorism through the use of airplanes. Other than the chance of a hijacking, which I thought would probably happen in a foreign country, the thought never occurred to me that this type of violence would happen in America. Immediately after the attacks, I felt that I would only fly if it were an emergency and that was the only way I could reach my destination in the time needed for the emergency. Post-September 11th, I feel that anything is possible anywhere when individuals make up in their minds that they are going to make a statement by doing any type of violent endeavor."

- "Before the attack, I felt that airport security was adequate, never ever considered a terrorist act would occur, and felt safe. After the attack, I did not want to board a plane ever again since I did not know the facts and details on the security breach, those responsible, or how the government was going to prevent this...Now, I am very cautious, appear to be ready to notice the peculiar behavior or sudden need to duck for cover."

- "In my opinion, 9/11 made it more difficult for anyone who wants to hijack an airplane to a different destination (the old mode of hijacking). Nowadays, anyone causing a ruckus on an airplane is likely to be beaten into submission by the other passengers, who will be willing to fight to the death."

- "Before, I felt secure. Immediately after, I felt angry. Now, I feel concerned and frustrated."

- "Before, I had no significant problems with security. Immediately after, I did not want to fly, mainly because of the hassles. Now, no change."

- "I have an aviation background, so before 9/11 I had no problem. I would climb on an airplane, kick the tires, shake the wing, and take off. It wouldn't make any difference. Post 9/11, I didn't want to fly. Now, it's a hassle."

In addressing this issue, we are still at Step 2 of Booth-Butterfield's consistency theory—a state of dissonance. We have identified the problem, and we should be moving toward Step 3, which states that dissonance drives us to restore consistency.

Given that dissonance is an unpleasant experience, when we have it, we want to get rid of it. We want to get back to the state of consistency—back where things made sense and we didn't have that awful dissonance. No matter the method, we must lose the dissonance and restore consistency. Air travelers want that sense of security again and not just a warm and good feeling. When they walk into an airport in Washington DC or Atlanta, Georgia, they want to see the same level of safety and security measures taken regardless of how big or small the facility.

Again, the focus is on leaders and leadership. According to Bernard M. Bass and Bruce J. Avolio (1994), leadership is regarded as the single most critical factor in the success or failure of institutions. Leaders in the airline industry must be proactive. They cannot sit back and wait for change. As clearly articulated by one individual from the research, "The reason you hear us addressing leaderships that this issue requires leadership, setting examples, pulling everybody together, doing the analysis, making the tough decisions, standing up, and taking charge." Leaders also need to be transformed to adapt to their organizations and environment. Bass and Avolio explained that transformational leadership occurs when leaders broaden and elevate the interests of their employees, when they generate awareness and acceptance of the purposes and the mission of the group, and when they stir their employees to look beyond their own self-interest for the good of the group. In applying this to the airline industry, leaders of their respective organizations are better able to gain a sustainable competitive advantage by changing the structure or composition of the market. Certains changes can be made without any assistance from federal agencies or outside organizations. This is what being transformed is all about—when industry leaders look beyond their own self-interest for the good of the employees, the group, and the organization.

Contribution to Existing Literature

This book contributes to the study of airline safety and airline security. Currently, there is little research in this most important area. Several agencies and Web sites study safety and security regarding aircraft, aircraft worthiness, and aircraft accidents; but, to date, there have been no other studies on how the perceptions of passengers changed after September 11, 2001, in regard to airline safety and airline security, the factors that influenced the change in passengers' perceptions, and why these perceptions changed. My research is the first of its kind.

Conclusions

After researching, conducting the interviews, and focus study group, I have come to the following conclusions:

1. The perceptions of the airline industry as identified throughout this research will continue to have a lasting impact in the minds of travelers because of the constant and continuous coverage by the media when an accident happens.

2. We must have consistency, and the airline industry must standardize safety and security measures across the United States.

3. Immediately following 9/11, passengers were more vigilant than they are today. My research shows that they are becoming complacent in the years since the attacks. I believe that this is a dangerous trend that airline leaders must acknowledge

Where Should Our Leaders Go from Here?

1. Leadership in the federal government, the FAA, and their supporting agencies should continue to work to change those procedures that were identified in the course of this research.

2. There is a need to expand the study of this research on a larger scale. There appears to a problem with unfair perceptions and flaws in the airline industry.

3. There must be standardization of safety and security measures at different airports. Safety and security measures must be consistent throughout the industry.

4. It is important to identify the role of the Transportation Security Administration (TSA) throughout this process. (The TSA protects the nation's transportation systems to ensure freedom of movement for people and commerce.) The TSA was not the focus of this research; but, several times in this research, travelers expressed concerns about some of the agency's inconsistencies and unprofessional behavior.

5. It is important to develop a more intelligent software system including a predictive analytic software tool that will allow the identification of suspect personnel before they pass through security. This may involve some element of profiling; but, if it helps deter another attack, some element of profiling may be worth the cost."

Closing Thoughts

Improving airline safety and security is one of the most urgent issues facing this nation and the world today. Though we are making progress in this industry in regard to safety and security, there appears to be the perception that travelers want to revert back to a pre 9/11 mindset. Travelers are becoming irritated with time-consuming airport security procedures and do not think this is necessary now. In their minds this was a necessary to perform immediately after the attacks.

This research answered three questions. First, how have passengers' perceptions of airline safety and airline security changed since September 11, 2001? Second, what factors have influenced the change in passengers' perceptions? Third, why have these perceptions changed? In the conduct of this research, additional questions were raised, and the respondents addressed them.

Throughout the course of the interviews and the focus study group, there was a constant theme—leadership. Leadership is paramount in every organization. According to Munroe (1993), leadership is the organizing and coordinating of resources, energies, and relationships in a productive context for an intended result. In its simplest forms, leadership is the managing of managers toward a common goal. Therefore, leadership, by its very nature, incorporates a clear purpose and vision that provide the fuel for inspiration, motivation, and mobilization.

Our government officials along with our leaders in the airline industry today are faced with many complicated issues in regards to the airline industry. By taking charge of the issues, addressing these issues, and leading from the front, they will restore the flying public's faith and confidence in the airline industry.

References

Air Transport Association. 2005. *What is the ATA? The ATA is the Air Transport Association of America.* http://www.airlines.org/about/d.aspx?nid=978 (accessed November 11, 2005).

Anderson, J.A. and Fulton, S.D. 2002. Tighter air control. Mechanical Engineering, New York, 38-41.

Ansoff, I. H. 1983. *Strategic management.* London: Macmillan.

Bass, B. M. 1990. *Bass & Stogdill's Handbook of Leadership: Theory, Research, and Managerial Applications.* 3rd ed. New York: Free Press.

Bass, B. M., and Avolio, B. J. 1994. *Improving organization effectiveness through transformation leadership.* Thousand Oaks, CA: Sage.

Booth-Butterfield, S. 1988. *Consistency. Klong! That does not compute.* http://www.as.wvu.edu/~sbb/comm221/chapters/consist.htm (accessed October 16, 2003).

Charan, R. 1991. How networks reshape organizations for results. *Harvard Business Review, 69,* 104-115.

Cherry, B. L. 2003. *Safety and security within the airline industry.* (Available from the Industrial College of the Armed Forces, National Defense University, Washington, DC 20319)

Cherry, S. R. 2001. Is it safe to fly yet? *Insight on the News.* http://www.findarticles.com/m1571/47_17/80900385/p1/ article.jhtml (accessed March 21, 2003).

Claybrook, J. 2001. Three recent FAA aviation security regulations failed to adequately protect public. *Public Citizen.* http://www.citizen.org/pressroom/release.cfm?ID=845   (accessed March 21, 2003).

Dawson, S., and Manderson, L. 1993. *A manual for the use of focus groups.* Boston: International Nutrition Foundation for Developing Countries.

DePree, M. 1987. *Leadership is an art.* New York: Bantam Doubleday Dell.

Dooanis, R., and Sampson, A. 2000. The airline industry. *Columbia Electronic Encyclopedia.* Columbia University Press. http://www.columbia.edu/cu/cup/cee/cee.html (accessed March 21, 2003).

Federal Aviation Administration. 2001. *Aircraft safety and security: Report to Congress.* Washington, DC: Author.

Federal Aviation Administration. 2003. *A brief history of the Federal Aviation Administration and its predecessor agencies.* Washington DC: Author.

Fishbein, M., and Ajzen, I. 1975. *Belief, attitude, intention, and behavior: An introduction to theory and research.* Reading, MA: Addison-Wesley.

Hahn, R. W. 1997. The economics of airline safety and security: An analysis of the White House Commission's recommendations. *Harvard Journal of Law and Public Policy, 20*(3), 791-827.

Hambrick, D. C., and Mason, P. 1984. Upper echelons: The organization as a reflection of its top managers. *Academy of Management Review, 9,* 193-206.

Helmreich, R., Kanki, B., and Wiener, E. 2002. *Cockpit security: FAA strengthens cockpit security.* http://www.yenra. com/cockpit-security/ (accessed March 21, 2003).

Isisdore, C. 2005. *Delta, Northwest file for bankruptcy: Spike in jet fuel sparks filings, putting almost half of U.S. airline capacity in Chapter 11.* CNN Money, http://money.cnn.com/2005/09/14/news/fortune500/ bankruptcy_ airlines/ (accessed November 11, 2005).

Kimhi, S., and Even, S. 2003. Who are the Palestinian suicide terrorist? Jaffe Center for Strategic Studies. http://www.tau.ac.il/ jcss/sa/v6n2p5Kim.html (accessed November 11, 2005).

Levin, A. 2002. Plan to arm pilots is taking off. *USA Today.* http://usatoday.com/ (accessed October 16, 2002).

Munroe, M. 1993. *Becoming a leader: Everyone can do it.* Lanham, MD: Pneuma Life.

Neilsen, E. H., and Hayagreeva Rao, M. V. 1987. The strategy-legitimacy nexus: A thick description. *Academy of Management Journal, 12,* 523-533.

Pearce, J. A., II. 1995. A structural analysis of dominant coalitions in small banks. *Journal of Management, 21*(6), 1075-1095.

Pearce, J. A., II, and David, F. 1983. A social network approach to organizational design-performance. *Academy of Management Review, 8,* 436-444.

Pearce, J. A., II, and DeNisi, A. 1983. Dominant coalition formation as interpreted through attribution theory. *Academy of Management Journal, 26,* 119-128.

Pennings, J. M. 1981. Strategically interdependent organizations. In P. D. Nystrom & W. H. Starbuck (Eds.), *Handbook of organizational design.* London: Oxford University Press.

Pfeffer, J. 1981. *Power in organizations.* Marshfield, MA: Pittman.

Pfeffer, J., and Salancik, G. R. 1978. *The external control of organizations.* New York: Harper & Row.

Pondy, L. R., and Mitroff, I. 1979. Beyond open systems models of organizations. In B.M. Staw & L. L. Cummings (Eds.), *Research in organizational behavior* (pp. 3-40). Greenwich, CT: JAI Press.

Priem, R. L. 1990. Top management team group factors, consensus, and firm performance. *Strategic Management Journal, 11,* 469-478.

Scott, W. A. 1967. *Organizational theory: A behavioral analysis for management.* Homewood, IL: Irwin.

Thompson, J. D. 1967. *Organizations in action*. New York: McGraw-Hill.

Ward, R. 2002. *September 11 and the restructuring of the airline industry*. http://www.dollarsandsense.org/ (accessed March 21, 2003).

Wassink, J. R. 2003. *Aircraft safety, security and aircraft design options*. (Available from the Industrial College of the Armed Forces, National Defense University, Washington, DC 20319)

Wassink, J. R., and Cherry, B. L. 2003. *Aircraft safety and security: Aircraft industry study report and presentation to the FAA*. (Available from the Industrial College of the Armed Forces, National Defense University, Washington, DC 20319)

Writing Center at Colorado State University. 2003. *Case study introduction and definition*. http://writing.colostate.edu/references/research/casestudy/pop2a. cfm (accessed November 13, 2003).

Yeoman, B., and Hogan, B. 2002. Airline Insecurity. *Mother Jones Interactive*. http://www.findarticles.com/cf_0/m1329/1_27/81515928/p1/article. jhtml?term= (accessed January 11, 2002).

Young, S. W. 1992. Educational experiences of transformational leaders. *Nursing Administration Quarterly, 17*, 1.

978-0-595-36398-8
0-595-36398-9

Printed in the United States
141529LV00004B/95/A